Hidayat Inayat-Khan

Path of Remembrance

Teachings on the Singing Zikar
of Hazrat Inayat Khan

Hidayat Inayat-Khan

Path of Remembrance

Teachings on the Singing Zikar of Hazrat Inayat Khan

Inayat-Khan, Hidayat

Path of Remembrance
Teachings on the Singing Zikar
of Hazrat Inayat Khan

Zürich: Edition Petama Project, Zürich, 2008

Published by: Petama Project, Puran Füchslin
                            Kanzleistrasse 151, 8004 Zürich
                            Email: puran@petama.ch
                            www.petama.ch

Concept and layout: Petama Project, Zürich

Production: Books on Demand GmbH
                            Norderstedt - www.bod.ch

1. Edition by Petama Project
Copyright © 2008 Hidayat Inayat-Khan

ISBN 978-3-907643-05-1

CONTENTS

PREFACE   6

O SUFI, DID YOU KNOW...   9

1.   THE EXTERNAL ZIKAR   10

2.   „COME IN THE TEMPLE OF MY HEART "   14

3.   BASIC INSTRUCTION IN THE SINGING ZIKAR   17

4.   „HOW DOES ONE PREPARE ONESELF?"   24

5.   ZIKAR   30

6.   THE SINGING ZIKAR   40

7.   WITHOUT ANY WANT OR DESIRE   48

8.   CONES OF LIGHT AND SOUND   52

9.   THE MYSTICAL GEOMETRY OF THE ZIKAR OF HAZRAT INAYAT KHAN   58

10.   THE CHROMATIC ZIKAR   71

PREFACE

Zikar is a spiritual practice at the heart of Sufism, in which the ancient syllables „La El La Ha, El Al La Hu" are rhythmically repeated, usually to the accompaniment of the head and body. The phrase may be loosely translated as: „God alone exists, none exists save He". The first part of the formula „La El La Ha" is a surrender, through which the seeker hopes to put aside the illusion of captivity. The second part of the Zikar, „El Al La Hu", confirms the all-pervading Divine Presence.

Taken together, the two parts of the phrase encapsulate the Sufi point of view, which has no particular dogma, seeing Truth hidden in all forms and in all beings. Therefore, the Sufi respects all religions and all forms of worship, knowing them to be inspired by the same divine source.

The focus of the Zikar is the heart; the heart-centre has been called the gateway to the soul, or the altar in the temple of God. The practice of Zikar strikes repeatedly on this centre, striving to make the spark of love blaze up brightly. By this the Zakir, the one who practices Zikar, becomes more pliant and responsive to the life within and around. In the words of Hazrat Inayat Khan: „The expression of the countenance becomes harmonious, the voice becomes melodious, the presence becomes healing... There is nothing that by Zikar cannot be accomplished..."

There are many kinds of Zikar, varying in melody and movement. Here we wish to present the Zikar taught by Hazrat Inayat Khan, who brought the Sufi Message to the West. This Zikar is the fruit of deep mystical insight and high musical attunement. It uses ancient words, set to a melody given specifically by our Master by this practice, for this age. To this are added traditional movements and visualisations, so that the whole forms a richly resonant experience in which, hopefully the illusion of separate identity dissolves in the consciousness of the Divine Presence.

This book is meant to offer some information and the insight of experience to those who practice the Singing Zikar of Hazrat Inayat Khan. Zikar is taught orally, but it is hoped that these pages will help sustain the beauty, grace and dignity of this most precious practice, and perhaps open some doors. It is not meant to encourage any speculation about that which one does not know, nor to stimulate displays of spiritual ,accomplishment'.

Zikar cannot be communicated through books any more than the colour of milk can be explained to one who cannot see it; direct experience is needed. If, however, one has done the Zikar even once, these pages may help one deepen in this practice. This collection of words and pictures is no substitute for one's own explorations, but it is offered in the sincere hope that it may be of some use on the journey.

Finally, it must be said that this book is the fruit of much love and many helpful hands, to whom grateful thanks are offered. First of all must be mentioned Hidayat Inayat-Khan, whose instruction and encouragement in the practice of Zikar planted many seeds.

Nawab Pasnak,
Sufi Movement Canada

A first publication of this book was edited in 1999, the author of the book, Hidayat Inayat-Khan, had worked together with Sufi students in Canada for many years, and so a first publication came about.

In the course of the translation into German the Petama Project re-edits this English version of the book, with the support and kind agreement of the author.

Zürich, autumn 2008   *Puran Füchslin*

OH SUFI, DID YOU KNOW...

that „Brotherhood and Sisterhood"
is the ship in which we are sailing
on the great waters
of Love, Harmony and Beauty;
guided by the compass
of the Spirit of Guidance,
and driven by the energy of Spiritual Liberty;
heading towards the goal of the annihilation of ego,
where one may begin at last to realize
that the sailor is verily the Divine Presence
sailing in the past, present and future
on the waves of our illusion.

Hidayat Inayat-Khan

1. THE EXTERNAL ZIKAR [*]

The External Zikar, which is silently inserted within the Sufi prayer „Saum", is to be understood as a preparation for the spiritual Sufi practice called Amal. The External Zikar is also practised as a special conditioning of the consicousness prior to all types of Zikar itself. This preparation stage is seen as an attunement to the awareness of oneself as an akasha within which the Divine Presence is manifesting.

---

[*]   *Hidayat Inayat-Khan - Leader's Retreat 1999*

It is important that all four stages of the
External Zikar practice is done with closed eyes.

STAGE ONE

When saying: „This is not my body, this is the temple of God",
one is mentally emphasising the reality of the Divine Presence, while
at the same time minimising the significance of the akasha. When
tracing a horizontal line, with three fingers, from left to right across
one's chest, one is feeling inspired to move onwards, from imperfection
to perfection. Then, when tracing a vertical line from the forehead
downward, one attunes oneself to the Prana channel along which the
Divine Presence is invited into the temple of one's heart.

For beginners, the eyes may be kept open in stage one,
especially when the practice is done collectively.

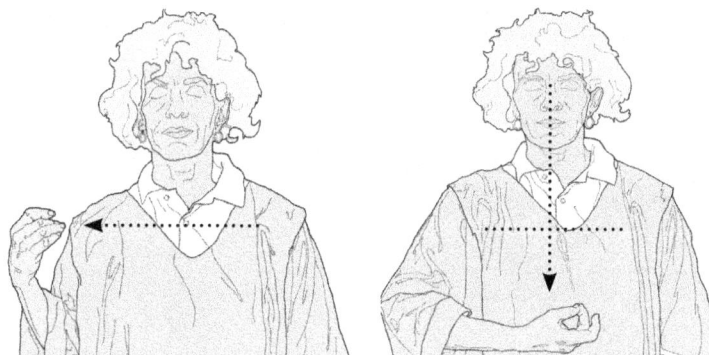

STAGE TWO

The second stage of the External Zikar practice is a psychological conditioning wherein one becomes conscious of the illusion of the self as compared to the all-pervading reality of the Divine Presence. In this stage, one visualises oneself as though standing outside oneself, while tracing upon the image of oneself the same lines as in stage one, but with the difference that this time, the palm of the hand is turned upwards while tracing the horizontal line (from the viewer's right to left) across the chest. The palm of the hand is stilll turned upwards when tracing the vertical line. This illusory reversed image of oneself symbolises the individual self as contemplated from a Divine perspective.

STAGE THREE

In stage three, one is still visualising oneself as though from without as in stage two, but the horizontal line from right to left and the vertical line from the forehead downwards are now traced mentally by the eyes in a relaxed and gentle movement of the head, instead of with a movement of the hand as in stages one and two.

STAGE FOUR

In stage four, the practice is done as a Fikar. Here the same cross is traced with the breath in co-ordination with the mentally recited words of the Zikar: „La El La Ha, El Allah Hu". The words „La El La Ha" in combination with the outgoing breath are pictured as an energy tracing a horizontal line going from the viewer's right to left across the envisioned image of oneself seen face to face. On the inhalation, the words „El Allah Hu" trace a vertical line from the forehead to the heart chakra. In stage four, it is advisable to first practice by sending the exhaled breath through the mouth on the words „La El La Ha". Later the exhaled breath is sent through the nose.

2. „COME IN THE TEMPLE OF MY HEART" *

Zikar is a very sacred experience. We know that the word ‚Zikar' means remembrance and we try to remember the Divine Presence as often as we can.

Now, there is the jelal Zikar, which is a very special mystical exercise, and which is prescribed by the initiators according to their feeling, understanding and sympathy towards the initiate. This jelal Zikar, which is perhaps, in different words, a ‚wazifa' Zikar, is the very positive repetition of an affirmation, which is „None exists save God, God alone is!" It is an affirmation; it is a conviction, and of course it is a tremendously powerful exercise, which is the reason why one should be very careful about the number of times that it is repeated.

---

*   Hidayat Inayat-Khan - Summer School Murad Hassil 1986

Aside from this jelal, ‚wazifa' Zikar, there is what we could call the jemal, ‚singing' Zikar, which is not that tremendously positive affirmation, but is the receptive aspect, the jemal aspect, calling the Divine Presence to come within the temple of the heart. In the jelal Zikar, where we have to do with an affirmation, the emphasis in Zikar one is on „El Allah Hu", which is also an affirmation: „God is!" and of course: „Hu".

In all these aspects of ‚wazifa' Zikar, the emphasis is on the downward movement upon the heart chakra, whereas in the Singing Zikar, which is jemal and receptive, the accent is different. It is „El," „come," „El Allah Hu." Where? In my heart. Therefore, the words have a different impact because it is directed towards the heart and it is a call for the Divine Presence.

Another aspect of meditation which we hope to elaborate here is that Zikar one, that is, the first part of the Singing Zikar, is a love song to God. It is just our heart opening to the Beloved. It is a love song, and it can only make sense if it is done with love. We plead for the Divine Beloved to come into our hearts. That is step two, a step further. There is the idea of duality here, the Beloved and my heart, so we have not yet reached the final ideal of the Zikar.

Zikar one is the love song to the Beloved, and Zikar two is an appeal for the Divine Presence to come into the temple of the heart. Zikar three is again one step further; God is responding, God is calling, saying: „But I am here in your heart; you did not see me but I was always there".

Now, coming to the real goal of Zikar: unless one does Zikar four, one is not really going as far as one should. Zikar, the meaning of Zikar, is to forget oneself in the Presence of the Divine. That is why Zikar four is so imporant, because one realises: „Yes, God is there but I am no longer there". The Beloved is there but the Lover is no longer there; there is only Beloved and Love.

3. BASIC INSTRUCTION IN THE SINGING ZIKAR [*]

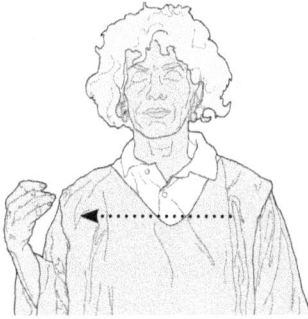

„This is not my body"   „This is the temple of God"

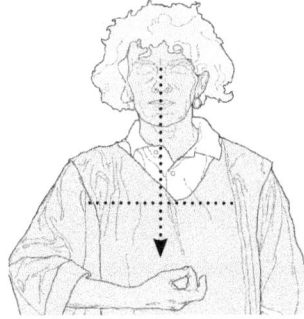

The usual preparation for the Singing Zikar is the External Zikar, repeated 11 or 33 times. As if holding a pencil of light with the right hand, one first traces a straight line from left shoulder to right shoulder, saying, „This is not my body". One then traces a vertical line, from the level of the crown down to the solar plexus, saying, „This is the temple of God".

The usual position for the Zikar is seated cross-legged on the floor. For those who find this position difficult, sitting on the edge of a chair is a good alternative. If possible, do not use the back of the chair for support, choose a chair with no arms so the body may move freely. The wrists should rest loosely on the knees. The right wrist is used to help push off for each rotation.

_____

[*]   Hidayat Inayat-Khan

The Zakir begins with the head bent toward the heart, and then describes a circle from the heart chakra to the right shoulder, up to the crown chakra and down into the heart chakra, remaining in the heart until beginning of the next phrase. This circle has its centre in the throat chakra.

la

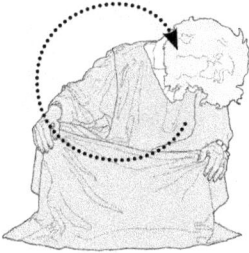

el Allah hu

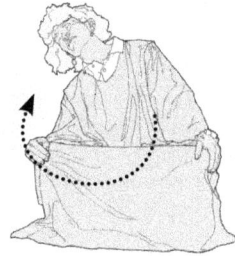

el la

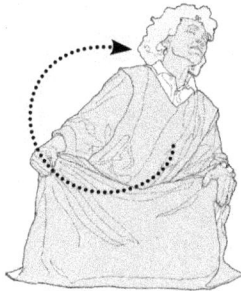

ha

In Zikar one the repeated phrase is „La El La Ha, El Allah Hu". The timing of the head movement is such that the head drops into the heart Chakra on the second „El".

el

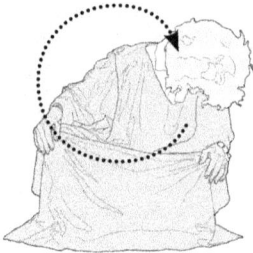

hu

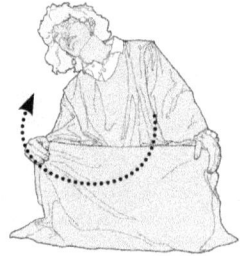

Al

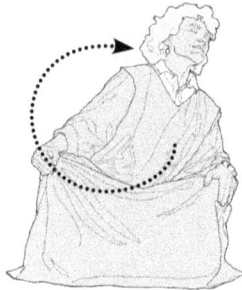

lah

In Zikar two the repeated phrase is „El Allah Hu". The timing of the head movement is such that the head drops into the heart Chakra on the last sound „Hu".

Al

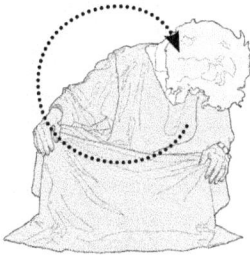

hu

la

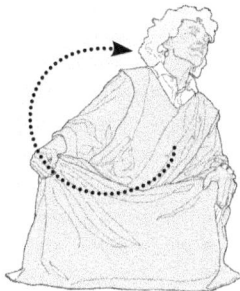

h

In Zikar three the repeated phrase is „Allah Hu". The timing of the head movement is such that the head drops into the heart Chakra on the last sound „Hu".

hu

In Zikar four the repeated phrase is „Hu". The timing of the head movement is such that the head drops into the heart Chakra on the last sound „Hu".

The movement of head and body is identical in each of the four parts of the Zikar. With the repetition of each phrase, there is a complete rotation.

The body moves in a circle, as if forming the shape of an inverted cone, the base of the spine being tip of the cone.

4. „How does one prepare oneself?" [*]

Question: What does a person do when arriving at the Zikar meeting? How does one prepare oneself?

Answer: It is obvious that, the Zikar being a most sacred communication with the Divine, those who come to the Zikar would like to come in clean clothes and with clean hands. Leaving behind, as far as it is possible, all negative vibrations and making every effort to make this Zikar meeting a coming together of brothers and sisters in one same family.

---

[*]   *Hidayat Inayat-Khan in an interview
       with Akbar Kieken at Rocky Mountain Sufi Camp 1983*

Question: Is it all right to socialise before the Zikar?

Answer: It is nice to have a little bit of something social before the Zikar, because during any type of communication between members of a centre coming to the Zikar meeting, by the very fact of talking to each other, they are more or less distancing themselves from any negative influences which they might bring with them. And somehow during this interchange between brothers and sisters prior to the Zikar, a harmonious situation is being established.

Question: What should the mental attitude of the individual be before starting the Zikar?

Answer: The attitude that is appropriate before starting the Zikar is brought about very beautifully when doing what Hazrat Inayat Khan called the External Zikar. This is a preparation in which one draws a horizontal line over the body with the fingers, saying „This is not my body," and then a vertical line from the forehead to the solar plexus, saying, „This is the temple of God." And while tracing this second line and saying, „This is the temple of God," one is trying to realise that this body is something sacred, and inasmuch as it is sacred, we should have respect for that temple.

Question: Why are we using recorded music? What is the purpose of the recorded accompaniment of the Singing Zikar?

Answer: There are two very important factors to remember when doing Zikar. One is to always keep the tone at a given pitch; the other is to keep the rhythm constant throughout. With the musical accompaniment of the recording, we are guided by the given constant tone, the background rhythm helps us tremendously all the way through.

Question: And why is it important that everyone be in the same rhythm?

Answer: Because we are building a network of energy, and in order for that network of energy to be realised, each element of it has to be in harmony with every other element. For instance, when one is building a temple of stone, one makes sure that all the stones used are, as far as possible, of the same size and type, so as to bring about a harmonious structure.

Question: Could you give us some idea of how the recording is used?

Answer: On this recording there are four parts: Zikar one, two, three and four. At the beginning of each one of these, there are three repetitions of the melodic formula of that particular part, which are given just to introduce the sound and the rhythm. Thereafter, on the fourth repetition, the rhythmic accompaniment begins, and we may start and go on guided by that melodic formula and rhythmic pattern all the way through. At the end of each one of these Zikars, the next to last repetition is marked with a bell, and the very last repetition is slower.

Question: Where are the accents in the four parts of the Singing Zikar?

*Answer: In Zikar one, the accent is on the first syllable of the second part of that sentence, as follows: „La El La Ha, **El** Allah Hu". As to the three others, Zikar two, Zikar three and Zikar four, the accent is just only on the **Hu**.*

26

Question: Could you please talk a bit about the significance of each of the four parts of the Singing Zikar?

Answer: Each time we diminish the length of the phrase of the Zikar, we are expressing more profoundly the essential message that the Zikar has to offer. The first Zikar is composed of the phrase, „La El La Ha", which means something like, „None exists save God," followed by „El Allah Hu," which means „God alone is". Zikar two is the words, „El Allah Hu," which means again „God alone is". Zikar three says, „Allah Hu," which means „God is," and Zikar four says „Hu," which really means, „Is," „All is," and nothing else „is." And when pronouncing the sound „Hu," which is the basic tone of the universe, one must try to attune oneself to the vibration which that sound is really building up. And each time that we pronounce that sound, it is like striking a hammer on a gong, after which the sound produced goes on vibrating forever in the universe.

Question: Could you say something about the rotation in the Singing Zikar, because it seems to be different from some other Zikars?

Answer: During the rotation, not only the head but the entire trunk is also in motion. Then, as to the direction, the rotation starts from the head chakra, goes upwads towards the right shoulder, then all the way up and finally comes back down into the heart centre.

Question: Is there some visualisation that we can keep in mind while doing the Zikar?

Answer: While doing this rotation, one could try to trace with the closed eyes a luminous circle which has as its centre the heart chakra. In other words, to see the rotation being inscribed all around one, illuminated by a luminous circle that we are tracing with our eyes closed.

Question: Could you say a little bit about the breath?

Answer: The breath in Zikar is extremely important, because while Singing Zikar, we are exhaling, and the louder we sing these Zikars, the more air is being exhaled. This is none other than a type of purification excercise, because not only are we exhaling but we are also throwing off all negative vibrations, such as those that build up self-consicousness. Now, in Zikar four, where the „Hu" is done on six beats, we have the opportunity of exhaling the maximum amount of air while pronouncing the sound „Hu," and at the same time making all possible efforts for that sound to resound in the heart chakra as the echo of a gong.

Question: And what is the meditation during the Singing Zikar?

Answer: The meditation during Zikar is of course the realisation of the words that we are pronouncing, which is to say, „La El La Ha, El Allah Hu", meaning „None exists save He, God alone exists." And after having repeated this formula several times, we go on doing it automatically in our minds, after which there comes a time that we can really meditate on what those words mean without having to force the presence of those words upon our minds.

Question: What happens when thoughts intrude into meditation, as so often happens?

Answer: There are several ways of combating thoughts which might come into one's mind while doing ZIkar, but one of the most positive methods is to lead one's mind back on to the track of the luminous circle just mentioned.

Question: What do we do when the Zikar practice has come to an end?

Answer: After the Zikar, it is most advisable to have silence for a minimum of ten minutes, during which one can try to recall in one's mind the sound „Hu," which goes on resounding in one's whole being, particularly in the chakras, as well as in the space where the Zikar has been performed. One can try to retrace the luminous circle if one has been mentally drawing it while doing the rotation, and that circle tends to become smaller and smaller until it ends up by becoming a flash of light, which one sees shining above the head chakra. In other words, the most effective result of the Zikar is that one goes on hearing the sound „Hu" resoundig in the heart chakra, and one goes on seeing the tremendously bright light. Even days afterwards, one might catch oneself hearing the sound „Hu," and seeing sparks of that bright light.

5. ZIKAR [*]

Zikar ist the process of repeating the sacred words as a meditation, that the meaning of the words may be impressed on the entire self. The Vedanta has called this process „Mantra Yoga" or „Jap." The Sufis have in all ages given great importance to this, for it is not only the thought but also the vibration of the sacred words combined with the motion of the body which makes perfect concentration. For a sincere disciple it does not take more than six weeks to discover its effect upon the self. It is wonderful in its power of giving inner realisation.

---

[*]   Teachings of Hazrat Inayat Khan, interpreted by Hidayat Inayat-Khan

Shams Tabriz says in this respect, „Allah, Allah, say Allah, and Allah thou wilt become; again I assure thee that Allah wilt thou surely become." The most truly spiritual people in the world have always attached the greatest importance to repeating the Name of God, for Zikar, being just that, is a sure method of spiritual progress.

THE VALUE OF REPETITION

Many consider it very monotonous to say the same thing over and over, to repeat the same word, to think the same thought, but they are utterly unaware of its benefit. Every time that a sacred word is repeated it has added power or illumination for whatever purpose it may have been meant. Repetition may be seen as the source of the success of a singer and of the skill of an artist. Each time the singer repeats a song, he gains more mastery; the more time the artist devotes to his work, the better is the result. What is more, the further one progresses, the greater the progress shall be.

There are people who have repeated sacred words for forty or fifty years of their life; and every year the words has brought deeper inner realisation., There are some who have realised progress through Zikar every moment of their life.

MUSIC OF THE SINGING ZIKAR

The Singing Zikar has a particular distinction when compared to all other practices, for the Zikar re-echoes in both the body and mind, setting both the matter and spirit of the Zakir's being to rhythm. Music is rhythm and tone, and if they are both produced in one's body and mind through Zikar, the very being of the Zakir becomes musical. In „Sama", the musical assembly of the Sufis, the music has a great effect on the Zakir. In the music of Sufis, which is composed upon ragas, there is a special emphasis on rhythm to produce the desired effect upon the physical and mental being of the Zakir.

The one who is responsive to music is also awakened to all nature's music - in other words, to all that is beautiful - because of being fully alive. One who is not responsive to love and does not admire all the beauty that is around one is as dead, and the reason why one is not responsive is that one is unmusical - not in the sense of music which is played by musicians, but in the sense of the sublimity of nature's music.

The Sufi, therefore, calls music „Ghiza-i-Ruh", meaning „the food of the soul." The Zakir, the living one, in comparison with the unmusical, the dead one, is as a tree compared to a rock. The rock is firm and steady and apparently dead, while the tree is bending, moving, and constantly growing. For in motion is life; the motionless is lifeless.

By Zikar the countenance of the Zakir becomes harmonious; the voice becomes melodious; the presence becomes inspiring; and the Zakir spreads magnetism in the atmosphere. There is nothing that cannot be accomplished by Zikar, either a spiritual or a material purpose. Through Zikar some very exceptional souls have attained ideal perfection through the liberation of the self.

Rhythm

The regular working of the physical body contributes greatly to one's health, and regularity depends upon the purpose of the soul, which has been given the body as its vehicle. Generally, irregularity of sleep, or meals, or activity, or repose, sets the whole mechanism of the body in disorder; many illnesses come owing to lack of rhythm.

Zikar has a direct effect on the heart, at once setting it in rhythm, and the circulation of the blood also adopts a new rhythm, which is suggested by the Zikar. In other words, the physical body becomes rhythmic in every way, which is the necessary first step towards spirituality.

The spark of life

For thousands of years the mystics of the East have experienced and realised the power of sound and the mystery of repetition. When a master recommends to the disciple a word to be repeated so many hundred or so many thousand times, the disciple does it willingly. Some repeat one single sound or a sacred word for years, and sometimes all their life, without being tired of doing the same thing again and again. The result of this proves to them its value; every month and every year, by repeating the same word, the light of their spirituality increases.

Zikar has two dimensions: one is its energy or spirit, and the other is its akasha or matter. The spirit is the breath current, which should be naturally prolonged through each repetition of the Zikar.

The akasha of the Zikar is created by the repetition of the sacred words. The akasha is the fire element, and the breath current is life. When life manifests as fire, the heart naturally becomes warmer, and coldness which is the condition of many hearts, begins to vanish. Then the word, voice, atmosphere, glance and touch all express warmth, and the presence of the Zakir radiates warm vibrations. In time the Zakir begins to respond to every form and every being. This warmth makes the fire blaze up, and from it a flame springs forth that illuminates the path of the Zakir. Zikar is of special importance in the mystical training of the Zakir, and through Zikar a Sufi attains everything on earth and in Heaven..

DAILY PRACTICE

A tender-hearted person does not need Zikar very much - a hundred repetitions is sufficient; but where the love element is lacking, more is required. In that case as much as three hundred repetitions of the Zikar can be helpful. Normally Zikar is done once a day, but it can be done more.

POSTURE

There are four principal postures which may be adopted for the Zikar; in all of them, the hands rest lightly upon the knees. One is used in the Zikar and Fikar, and that is called the posture of the Cupid (related to the devotion of Bhakti yoga).

This posture has a special effect on the feeling heart; with it, the usual effect of the Zikar upon the Zakir is even greater. That posture is to sit cross-legged, placing the second toe of the right foot in the hollow behind the left knee, and the big toe of the right foot over the adjacent sinews. The influence that this posture has upon the heart is to make it responsive.

The second posture is simply to sit cross-legged. This helps one to have ease and comfort and inspiration and peace. This posture is the posture of the king (related to the mastery of Raja yoga), because it gives happiness and comfort and pleasure to those who are accustomed to sit cross-legged.

The third posture is sitting on the left heel with the right leg crossed over, and the right heel pulled as close as possible to the left ankle. This posture is that of the adept who gains self-control, and who practices self-discipline (related to the physical discipline and self-abnegation of Hatha yoga).

The fourth posture is the posture of the sage (used for meditation, known as the Samadhi posture), and that posture is to place each foot on the opposite thigh. It is a most difficult posture, but one which aids in realising inner peace.

Now, one might think, what is the reason? The explanation is that as the two legs are two currents going outward from the heart, as are the arms, by putting the feet on the thighs one is neutralising these currents, as one does when closing the hands. Consequently the heart, which is the sun, has no more channel through which to release its own energy. Therefore it becomes brighter and more luminous, and all that is latent in it is realised.

Four aspects of Zikar

There are four essential aspects of Zikar which must be made clear:

One is the clear and correct repetition of the Zikar, „La El La ha El Allah Hu", which should be uttered all in one breath. Every word must be pronounced distinctly and rhythmically.

The second aspect of the Zikar is to think of the meaning of the words and form. The inner meaning is the realisation that „This is not my body, this is the temple of God."

The third aspect of the Zikar is to listen with the inner ear, so to speak, to the sound that resounds in the solar plexus as a consequence of the repetition of the word El, awaking thereby its intuitive nature. When the doors of the heart are opeend, one's latent magnetic power becomes manifest and is expressed in one's voice and word and at-mosphere.

The fourth aspect of Zikar is to awaken a feeling of humility, „Why should I ever have thought I owned this property of my body which in reality does not belong to me?" This attitude makes Zikar even more living.

The proper pitch

In practising Zikar ones hould consider one's body as a harp, and the repetition of the words is like playing upon it, and one should hear the echo of one's own words resounding in the heart and head. First it vibrates in the heart, next it resounds in the head. Then it resound in the entire body. When this occurs, one must know that one's body is now tuned to a beautiful pitch. If the body is not prepared so, the mind and soul will be hindered in their expression of the Zikar.

Zikar is one of the most special mystical practices there is. This is so because there is a spark within a person, and when it is blown upon, as in this practice, it glows and bursts into flame. Warmth begins to radiate from a Zakir which is healing and consoling. The flame of intelligence blazes up in the Zakir, an intelligence which illuminates the path of the Zakir in the seen and unseen world. The more one becomes conscious of its effect, the more one is able to use it for the right purpose.

The only secret of understanding the full power awakaned by Zikar resides in directing it with wisdom. There is nothing in the world which appears unattainable to the one who has mastered Zikar.

SENSITIVENESS

Zikar makes the Zakir more sensitive to all things around him. It is because of this sensitivity that the Zakir must develop self-control and rise above all earthly passions, developing kindness and goodness, which, by the practice of Zikar, emanate from the Zakir's personality as perfume coming from the burning of incense.

THE HEART

The greatest and most important centre in the human body is the heart. One often expresses love, sorrow and joy by pressing one's hand to the breast. This shows that every kind of feeling first strikes the heart. The heart being the origin of all feelings, it has its influence upon the whole body.

By the practice of Zikar, this centre is wakened both by vibrations and by the magic touch of Prana, which brings life. One then begins to understand the meaning of the heart being like a mirror. It is the sensitiveness of the heart which gives it the mirror-like quality. When it is not awakened, it is like a clouded mirror. This mirror is two-sided, one side reflecting that which is within, and the other that which is without. The wise are able to differentiate the importance of one side of the mirror from the other, by covering one side in order to observe the reflection in the other. Once the heart is cleared from all negative vibrations, it becomes a living presence, capable of receiving the Message from within or without.

6. THE SINGING ZIKAR [*]

In the practice of the Singing Zikar, and we are speaking here only of the four part Singing Zikar of our Master, the rotation of the body from left to right is meant to be done in absolute harmony with the pattern of the rhythmically chanted raga. Of course the rhythm of these beats is different in each one of the four Zikars.

[*] Hidayat Inayat-Khan - Lecture at Lake O'Hara 1990

Furthermore, every effort must be made to keep the voice in pitch, so that the vibrations of the sounds produced can awaken resonances to specific tones within the chakras, awakening at the same time heightened consciousness. For this reason, it is most advisable to be guided by a recording, which certainly helps in maintaining the proper tone and rhythm. It is a paradox, of course, but the truest freedom is only awakened within the boundaries of self-discipline. However although we may avail ourselves of the material assistance of tapes, musical instruments or metronomes, it must be understood that Zikar is the cry of the heart, the yearning of the soul; and eventually, like the flying carpet of fairy tales, Zikar carries one right up into heaven, with the help of its magic beauty.

While expressing the divine music of God's Presence, inspired by the Spirit of Guidance, one's innermost wish might be to interpret that music harmoniously, so that it may resound as beautifully as possible within one's heart as a sacred message of love, human and divine. However, love is only really experienced to the extent the „I" is no more there. As it is said, in the heart there is only place for one, either the self or the Beloved.

Before practicing the Zikar itself, our master strongly recommended that the mind should be prepared or conditioned by the External Zikar. This is done by tracing a horizontal line from left to right across the chest with the index finger of the right hand, while saying, „This is not my body." Then, tracing a vertical line from the forehead as far as the heart chakra, we say, „This is the temple of God.

At a further stage, the same practice is done with closed eyes, while visualising a luminous line being traced by the eyes, as was done previously with the index finger. For still more advanced experience in these External Zikar practices, our Master has also suggested that one become the spectator, visualising oneself as if in a mirror, while tracing the horizontal and vertical lines.

We can note in passing that this same cross is also traced during the Sufi prayer „Saum." This is done with identical movements in the interval which occurs just after having said the words „Illuminate our Souls with Divine Light".

Now, coming to the subject of the Zikar practice itself (known to the Hindus as Japa yoga) it is worth noting that during this practice many different disciplines are being developed simultaneously. For instance, for physical discipline (hatha yoga) a chosen posture is useful. Mental discipline (jnana yoga) can be achieved with the help of various mind control methods. In meditation, the emotions are focussed on the evidence of the Divine Presence (bhakti yoga), ultimately losing the self in the folds of the Beloved (samadhi).

During the practice of Zikar, there are some technical considerations to be observed. For example, the ‚king' posture is recommended because the legs are relatively relaxed when sitting in a cross-legged position, although the ‚cupid posture' is known to be the most effective one for this practice. Nevertheless, there is no real obligation regarding the posture to be adopted. Some sit on chairs, providing that the rotation of the upper body is not hindered by the arms or the backs of the chairs.

Another point to consider is that in Zikar the hands should really be on the knees, to bear the weight of the upper body during the rotation movement, but leaving the fingers relaxed, so as to enable the free flow of magnetism while doing this very sacred practice.

The word ‚Zikar' means remembrance, remembrance of the Presence of God while losing oneself in the folds of a most sacred experience. It is the remembrance of a Divine Presence which no expression could ever describe, but which becomes a reality to the extent that one is prepared to forget the self, no matter how one is occupied. It is also the remembrance of the privilege we are offered in being able to share the reality of that Presence with all those with whom we come in contact, and who are consciously or unconsciously responsive to our words, thoughts and feelings, not to mention to the prana rays.

It is well known that the many variations of the Zikar practice have been in existence for centuries throughout the East. Whatever the form, though, it is important to remember that a Zikar can ultimately be either constructive or desctructive, depending upon the real purpose that one has when practising it. If practised to become highly spiritual or to become tremendously powerful, even the very best Zikar of all can turn out to be a bad one. The mystical explanation of this paradox is that Zikar is not done to become something, it is done to become nothing.

Our Master has left us his own Zikar as a most sacred heritage. In this Zikar, the breath of the Message of today can be felt as a new impulse arising in the ever-present consciousness. The secret of the magic radiance of our Master's Zikar resides in the mystical co-ordination of a melodic raga with a constant rhythmic pattern, in accompaniment to sacred words offered as a humble invitation to the Divine Presence, within the temple of the heart.

Zikar one is the ‚love song', which is a song in itself; Zikar two is the yearning call for the Divine Presence; Zikar three is the tremendous feeling of happiness because the Divine Presence has answered the call and is becoming a reality in the depth of the heart; and Zikar four is that reality alone, when the self is no more there.

Each time we diminish the length of the sentence of the Zikar we are coming closer to the profound message that it has to offer. The first Zikar is the sentence, „La El La Ha", which means „no other God is", followed by „El Allah Hu", which means again „God alone is." Zikar two is based on the words „El Allah Hu", which means „God alone is". Zikar three says „Allah Hu" which means „God alone is," and Zikar four says „Hu", which really means „Is" or „All is" and nothing else „is". And in fact when pronouncing the sound „Hu", which is the basic tone of the universe, the all-pervading sound in space, the all-pervading light, one must try to come into that vibration. Each time we produce that sound, we are like a hammer on the gong, after which the sound produced goes on vibrating forever in the universe.

In Zikar, the breath technique is also very important. Along with the expelled breath, one is eliminating negative influences, while the positive vibrations of the sacred words have a purifying, revivifying and uplifting effect. The breath moves in harmony with the rhythm of the Zikar, and because of the regularity of the chanted repetitions, the breath automatically adopts a different rhythm. Through harmonising oneself to a different rhythm than one's own, one finds oneself as a spectator confronted with the limitations of all those identifications built up in one's mind by one's own false ego.

Another aspect of the breathing technique to consider is that, obviously, fluctuations in the breath and in the voice are necessary in order to emphasise the accents on certain words of the Zikar, while striking the chin upon the chest or heart chakra. This action has been illustrated in various ways by our Master; as hammering on a gong or a church bell; as cracking a hard nut; or as shooting an arrow at an inner target.

At a later stage of experience, the eyes trace a visualised lumious circle during each rotation of the Zikar. The centre of that circle is the heart chakra, and its diameter is the distance from the floor to the crown chakra. This visualised circle can be very helpful in controlling the mind. Obviously, during the practice of Zikar the concentration might tend to fade away, and as a remedy to this failure, our Master advised simply leading the mind back onto the circle of light. Soon enough, the mind returns automatically to that same luminous track of thought, back again under control and fully available for further meditation on the sacred words of the Zikar.

The main object of meditation during Zikar is to become attuned to the meaning and to the vibrations of the words „La El La Ha, El Allah Hu", none exists save God, God alone is. These very ancient words have been repeated millions and millions of times by countlesss enlightened souls, and have resounded in their hearts for ages and ages, accumulating whole worlds of magnetism, perceptible to all those who are receptive to the magic encountered each time that the sacred words of the Zikar are pronounced.

The after-effect of the Zkar is experiened while hearing the sound „Hu" constantly resounding within the heart chakra for days and days afterwards. That fascinating tone offers tremendous guidance in the attunement ot the secret vibrations of the Universe, which become thereby intelligible in the form of sound-waves of higher consciousness.

Along with this audible expression of the „Remembrance," there is also a visible aspect in the form of the lumious circle that has visualised during the Zikar practice, and which persists afterwards, gradually becoming smaller and smaller in one's mind, culminating in dazzling sparks of light flashing out into space. This silent „message of light" is only revealed to the extent that the effacement of the self has transcended into a love song of resignation to that Almighty Presence, the omnipresent source of all creation which is constantly pouring Divine Light into our hearts.

7. WITHOUT ANY WANT OR DESIRE [*]

„To be is not to be." Of course we all know that in the material world, if we want to get anywhere, the question is, „To be or not to be". But on the spiritual path, it is exactly the opposite. If we want to be spiritual, we shall never be it. Why? Because we are it already, but we don't know it. It's a paradox.

And perhaps we have experienced that in Zikar, one does tend to forget. The word Zikar means remembrance. Remembrance of what? Remembrance of the Divine Presence, and the more we want to be spiritual, the more we forget about the Divine Presence.

---

[*]   Hidayat Inayat-Khan - Rocky Mountain Sufi Camp 1986

There are hundreds of Zikars, perhaps even thousands, and they can all be good and they can all be bad. It is why we do Zikar which makes the Zikar either good or bad. If we do Zikar in order to be spiritual, it is better not to do it. Zikar means remembrance. But if we are trying to remember the Divine Presence, how can we be busy with ourselves, trying to make ourselves a spiritual person? This is a contradiction.

Let us recollect that Zikar is not done in order to accomplish anything; Zikar is not done for any benefit, be it material or spiritual. Zikar is not done in order to become anything, neither spiritual nor successful nor anything else. Zikar is not done for healing, nor for any accomplishment, nor for any desire at all. Zikar is only done as a practice which helps to forget that we even wanted to forget ourselves.

This is a wonderful point to remember: Sufism teaches us to use the ego for the right purpose. It teaches us to tame it, not to destroy it. Unfortunately some, with the hope of becoming spiritual, while doing Zikar are really thinking to themselves, „I alone exist, none exists save me". Zikar only makes sense if we forget our ego, and if we even forget that we wanted to forget. And the only way to forget that we wanted to forget is to place all our mind, our thoughts, our feelings upon the Divine Presence.

What follows now is very difficult to put into words. It is only when we forget that we wanted to forget ourselves, that we might all of a sudden be confronted with the Divine Presence. Doing Zikar four we might become consicous of the message which the sound „Hu" communicates when completely absorbed in its secret call. Even at various moments of the day or night, during our daily occupations or while resting, that universal sound resounds at unexpected occasions, as a result of which we become lost in the eternal „Hu." The sound of all planets, the sound of the universe, in fact the only sound there is, the sound of the Divine Presence.

If the word „sacred" ever had a definition, it would be just this: to forget that we wanted to forget ourselves, our egos. And all of a sudden we are confronted with the Divine Presence. Without any want, without any desire... and that is why, „not to be is to be". Because when one has no more desire, no more want, one is at-one with the Divine Presence.

8. Cones of Light and Sound [*]

In Zikar there are of course several geometrical concepts. As you know, you can place circle around all the chakras, a word which in any case means „wheel". Now all these circles exist within the akasha or capacity of two cones, set one on top of the other with their bases together. The point of the lower cone corresponds to the bottom of the spine, and the base, which is of course a circle, is at the level of the heart chakra.

---

[*]   Hidayat Inayat-Khan - in a conversation
       at Fazal Manzil, Suresnes, 1987

Then you have another cone, the circular base of which corresponds to that same heart chakra, and the point of which rises up through the top of the head. Now, you can make a cone just as small or as large as you want, so the cone which is on top should, for the charm of the picture and the sake of symmetry, be about the same size as the one that is underneath. Where they both meet is at the level of the heart chakra. When relating the size of those two cones to the size of a human being, the chakra of the top of the head would correspond more or less to half the height of the top cone, and the chakra of the abdomen would correspond more or less to half the height of the bottom cone. If these correspond more or less, then (since these chakras are identified as circles) these circles could of course be spinning within the cones.

But now things become more complicated. Every circle is in fact a section of a globe. In other words, if this is done correctly, what you would really see is chakras looking like planets rotating within these two cones, which, with a lot of imagination, could be seen to correspond to the solar system.

That is with regard to cones of light, but there are cones of sound, also, and these of course correspond to the sound one is producing when doing Zikar. When doing the Singing Zikar, the sound resounds not only in one's throat and chest but it also radiates from the ears. Especially in Zikar four, the eardrums are vibrating like kettle drums.

The more one is conscious of those cones, the more one also becomes conscious of the reality of the sound and light radiating from the chakras. In order to become conscious of something abstract, one has to base one's primary knowledge on something concrete. One has to first go through the concrete before coming to the real; one has to fix in one's mind the dimensions, the akasha or capacity of the sound and the light. Whether one sees it as a cone or a circle or a globe doesn't matter, but one has to first see it according to something of which one's mind can conceive. Then, the next stage is to see that akasha growing to a size which exceeds all limited conception. One first uses it as a framework in order to centralise one's mind according to a conceivable dimension, after which the consciousness can extend to an unlimited dimension.

Just as one fist concentrates on the physical discipline - sitting cross-legged and moving properly and all that, which are purely outward aspects of the concentration, in order that the consciousness may be free to fly about without being disturbed by any physical interruption - in the same way the mind must first be channelled through a certain discipline, a discipline of shape, of size, of direction, of anything that is conceivable, anything that can be intelligibly expressed, so that the next step can be one of absolute freedom in the abstract without being limited by dimension, size and proportion..

One has to first start by discipline before all the doors of freedom are opened. If you first start with freedom without discipline, that freedom just goes wild and goes astray. It cannot be functional. It cannot be operational..

The first geometry to concentrate upon during Zikar would be the two cones of light, whereby one's mind is directed to a certain dimension - a certain size, a certain form - through which it becomes more coherent, after which it can expand to larger dimensions. Then one might concentrate on the cones of sound. As soon as one starts singing, that sound resounds in the head and is channelled outward through the ears in a finer texture, developing into a cone shape. At the same time, the sound radiates down into the heart chakra and up above one's head. When one produces the sound „Hu" in Zikar four, one feels it in the ears, one feels it in the heart and one feels it in the head. If one can first conceive of these cones, one can understand that the oound which is starting from the centre is developing along definite lines. Once that is fixed in the mind, then it can be left to the unconscious to work further, and those cones become larger and larger until they don't really exist any more. And that is where the real meditation starts.

In concentration, the mind is limited to a shape, to a proportion, to a distance, to a concrete concept. Then even though the mind carries the imprint of a concept, those concepts can drop and the mind remains, all-pervading.

The cones can also be pictured going the other way. The sound is produced from the centre, comes out and strikes wherever it finds, and rebounds to the centre.

That is the idea of the mirror; in other word, whatever you can give corresponds to what you have received. You cannot give anything, either spiritually or materially, which you have not received.

So whatever you send out echoes back and it is with that re-echo that you can send it back again. In radio, the radio waves hit the ionosphere, and they reflect it back again, and what you hear is the echo of what strikes the ionosphere. In the same way one hears the re-echo of the „Hu" sound which was initially produced. One's energy spreads out, and strikes somewhere - instead of the ionosphere, perhaps it is the Divine Presence. it reaches the Divine Presence, and the returning echo offers one renewed strength.

That is what gives this idea of cones oriented in different directions, either originating in the heart or radiating towards the heart, which is all an example of the fundamental law of reciprocity experienced at various levels of the entire universe.

Why do we think the feeling is only within the heart? For example, the ear is stimulated by sound and that stimulation sends repercussions outward. So when one produces the sound „Hu", the heart becomes resonant and that innner resonance, (as distict from the outer resonance, which is the chant itself) of course also reaches the ear.

And what is the ear, really? The ear is nothing else than an extension of the brain, and through the sound vibration, the brain is automatically stimulated. In other words, by way of the ears, which only serve as the means of communication, the intensification of the longing in the heart produced by the sound is communicated to the brain.

Then there is yet another cone, with its point at the level of the ears and its base above the head, which is radiated by the brain. Any stimulation produces vibration, vibration produces light and then automatically the vibrations reach upwards toward finer spheres, making perceptible thereby the reality of the Divine Presence.

The process is so difficult to put into words, and one can only understand it when experiencing it. One produces energy, or more correctly one channels it outward - but that energy is not lost, it comes back again in a different way. there is always a constant reciprocal communication.

The eardrum vibrates in response to two different sets of stimuli, either from the exterior sound, or to sound from within. When you are producing the sound of Zikar, you are pressing that eardrum outwads, and this is when the physical idea of the cone makes sense. And of course, the result of it is the subtle pressure which produces intense vibrations on the brain which is then spinning out rays of light.

9. THE MYSTICAL GEOMETRY OF THE ZIKAR OF HAZRAT INAYAT KHAN *

The understanding of the practice of the Singing Zikar can be deepend by exploring both the ‚real‘ effects and the symbolic, metaphysical effects. This exploration is intended to link the literal experience with the figurative and hence unify man's Divine and material dual nature. It is not intended to be an explanation, which may very well be impossible, given the individuality of the experience. Zikar is a deep and profoundly mystical practice; the more it is explored the more one realises there is to explore.

---

*   David Murray

There is no wrong approach to understanding. If this serves to illustrate the mystical potential of Zikar, it will have performed its service.

The physical attributes of Zikar are: breath, rhythm, repetition, vibration and the word. Each of these attributes is a crucial ingredient in the practice of the Zikar. In spiritual traditions around the world, practices have been developed for each of these aspects; so they can be individually strengthened and made more useful in our everyday lives. In the Siging Zikar of Hazrat Inayat Khan, each attribute systematically supports and enhances the next, until they reach their completion in the final phase of the Zikar, Zikar four. The importance of these mystical attributes is expressed in these quotes here from the „Music of Life" by Hazrat Inayat Khan.

BREATH

„.....when we come to the mystery of breath, it is another domain altogether. The perceptible breath that the nostrils can feel as air drawn in and air going out is only an effect of breathing. It is not breath. For the mystic, breath is that current which carries the air out and brings the air in. The air is perceptible, not the current; the current is imperceptible. It is a kind of ethereal magnetism, the current of which goes in and comes out, putting the air into motion".

„...to the mystic, breath is like a lift, a lift in which he rises up to the first flor, and then to the second, and then to the third floor - in fact to whatever level he wishes to reach."

Rhythm

„Rhythm is the main aspect of breath, as it is on the rhythm of the breath that the working of the whole mechanism of our being depends."

„Evenness of rhythm is balance, while unevenness is a lack of balance. The harmony in rhythm develops the beauty of human character."

Repetition

„In ancient languages words came into being by inspiration. Modern languages are based on the logical reasoning of the grammar one learns. Certain words that have come purely by inspiration and that adapted in harmony with man's experience in daily life are more powerful than the words of the languages we speak today. Thus they have a greater power when repeated, and a great phenomenon is produced when one has mastered those word."

„Each vowel has its psychological effect. The sages use special words that they repeat in the morning or in the evening, and by this there is a certain illumination, a certain state of exaltation. It is this very mystery which the Sufis of ancient times practised as Zikar. This is the method of bringing about desirable results when repeating the proper words or phrases."

VIBRATION

„Correct breathing brings the mind into harmony with the subtle vibrations of the universe. The more intensely the life innerly manifests, that much more perceptible are the vibrations thereof. "

„It is the vibrations set in motion by the breath that become thought waves that transmit thoughts from one mind to the other."

THE WORD

„Wisdom is the result of an understanding at an inner level of experience, whereas intellect is the accumulation of outer knowledge. However, both have the same origin, which the mystics of all times have described as being the original word. The Sufis of all ages have therefore given the greatest importance to the word, knowing that the word is the key to the mystery of the whole life, the mystery of all planes of existence... the principal and central theme of mysticism is the word"

THE EFFECTS OF THE SINGING ZIKAR

The effects of the Singing Zikar are:

Rotation, which is the result of the attributes of breath, repetition and rhythm.

A rising effect, which is the result of the previous attributes combining to generate the vibration of the Zikar.

Transformation from denseness to lightness, which is the result of the attributes of vibration and the Word.

The following drawings and words will help to explore the effects of the practice of Zikar and the ultimate purpose for which Zikar has been given.

• The dot is the geometric expression of the symbolic source of all, unity, the divine.

The circle derives from the dot and symbolically expresses multiplicity.

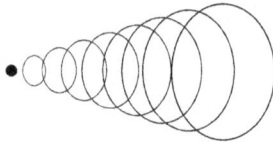

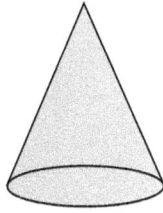

In three dimensions, the cone geometrically expresses the relationship between the material and the Divine.

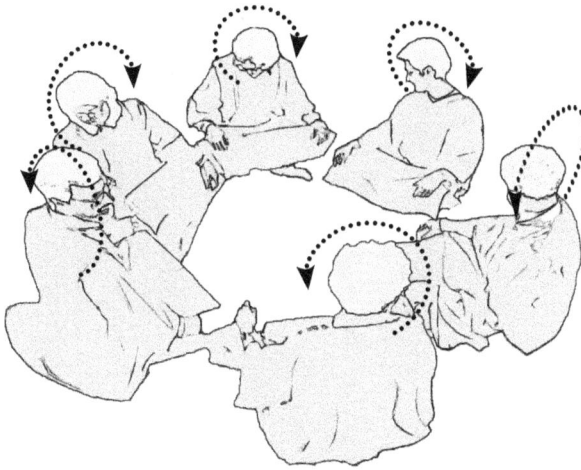

The form of the practice of Zikar is the circle. The action of the Zikar practice is the counter-clockwise movement of the heads of the participants or Zakirs sitting in a circle.

This rotating activity generates the effect of a counter-clockwise movement around the sitting circle.

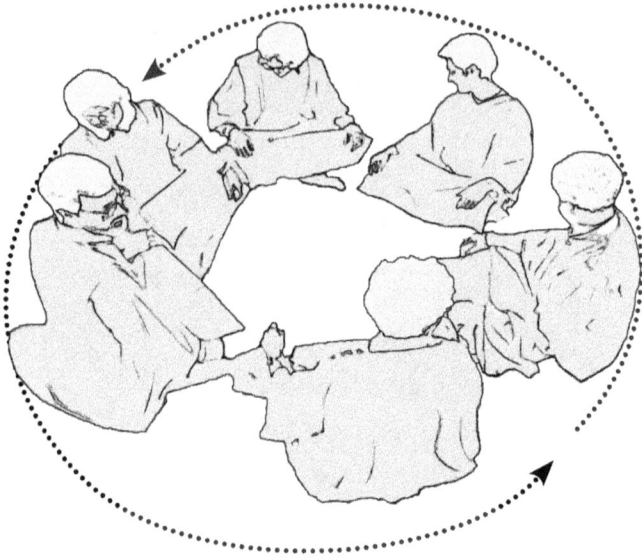

The rotational effect can be anticipated and initiated through the counter-clockwise walk which can commence the Singing Zikar.

The effect of the motions of rotation and rising is to create the motion of an upward moving spiral.

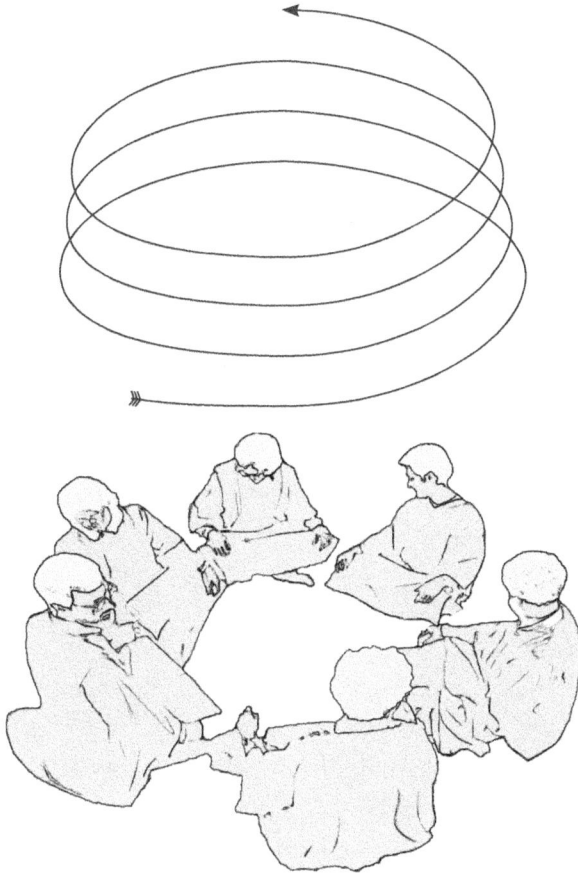

The action of the Zikar and the repetition of the Zikar phrases develop a regular breath among the Zakirs.

The breath, in combination with the synchronised body movements, develops the attribute of rhythm which is a musical concept signifying the joining of independent actions to create a single effect. The effect is the vibration of the Zikar, which can be imagined as a mystical entity or ‚life force' representing, through the collaborative actions of the group, the concept of unity.

After the repetition of the head and body movements, all emphasis is on the repetition of the Zikar phrases and especially the sound „Hu." The effect of the vibration of the Zikar in combination with the word generates the great mystical transformation which makes Zikar such an important and useful practice. The effect is liek that of an electrical generator. With each repetition of the word (sound) „Hu," one can imagine a spark of light being generated. The source of this energy is that which is drawn up from the material plane and the direction of this energy movement is upward, in a spiral, the result of the circular rotation.

In the geometry of the Zikar, the sitting circle can be considered as a circular plane, the plane of transformation.

The generated light rises in a spiral pattern. To express the concept of unity, which is the purpose of the vibrational ‚being', the upward moving spiral decreases to a single point. A geometrical cone is created. The base represents the plane of transformation and the peak of the cone represents unity, or the Divine.

When expressed as geometry, the form of Zikar is a gradually evolving cone of light, the spiral ever decreasing and rising toward the symbol of the divine ideal, the point at the top of the cone.

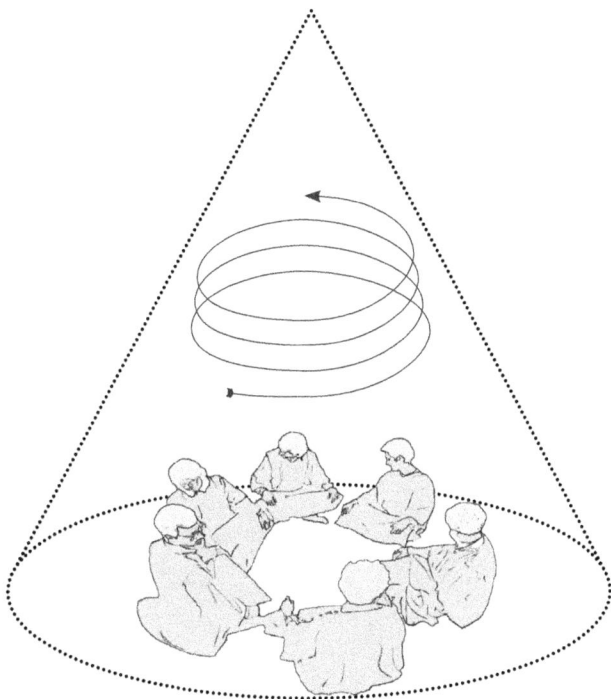

The geometrical expression is not complete until that which is drawn up from below has been graphically represented. The form of multicplicity, the material, can be expressed by an inverse cone below the cone of transformation. The two opposite points represent the perception of duality. The lower cone can be imagined to be solid.

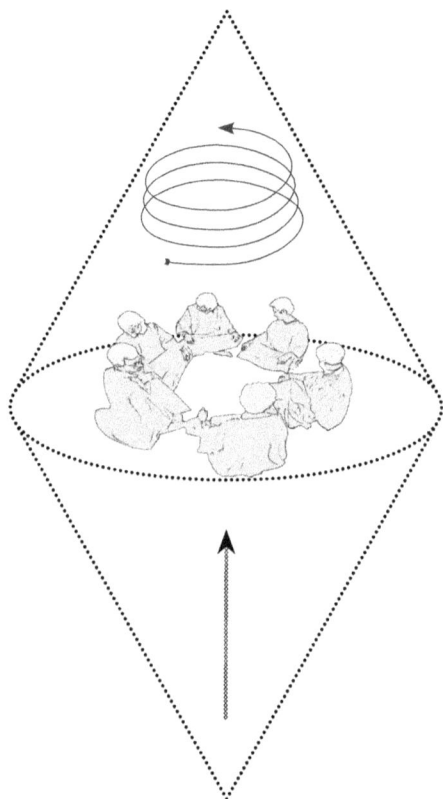

The cone and the point at its lowest end represent the limitation of the material realm. It also represents the perception of duality. As the Zikar is performed, the upper cone fills with light from above. The lower cone loses its solidity as it is converted into light.

Eventually the entire geometrical structure is filled with light and becomes the only entity.

The light-filled geometry expresses the purpose and resul tof the practice of Zikar - that is, the unification of the Divine and the material. The process by which this is achieved illustrates that the Divine Presence is nothing but the light that is already in all forms, hidden by the mask of our ego. The practice of Zikar releases this light an dilluminates our consciousness. The Divine Presence is invoked by our own actions. Each individual is a channel for the Divine.

„Disclose to us Thy Divine Light"

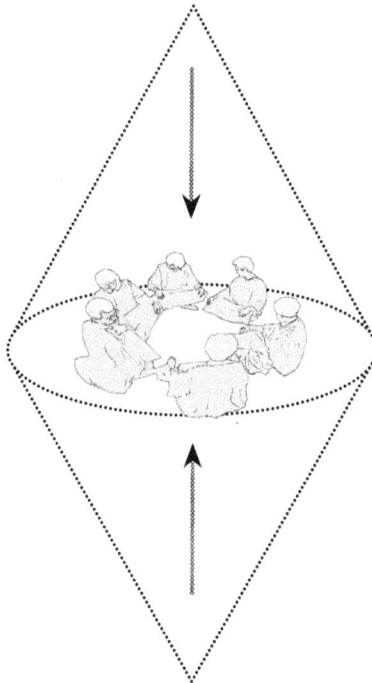

„Raise us from the Denseness of the Earth"

In summary, this geometric exploration is intended to serve as a mechanism to help individuals come to a deeper understanding of this ancient practice. It is intended specifically to assist the rational part of our consciousness to melt with the intuitive so that the full effect of the Zikar practice can be realised.

The geometry developed here is quite simple. It is up toteh individual to explore the geometric forms more deeply, if so desired, so that the experience is personalised. There is only one simple lesson to be learned from this exercise and thatis that we as individuals have the capacity for deep and complete divine Realistaion. We are the channels and we are the Light. Collectively, the practice of Zikar is a shared experience on a higher plane of consciousness. It is an effective means by which Sufis can manifest their innermost longing for uni-fication with the Divine. Zikar intensifies every human potential, the potential of the heart and the potential of the mind.

10. THE CHROMATIC ZIKAR *

Finally we come to the Chromatic Zikar practice, which is so valuable because it develops so many things at the same time.

---

*   von Hidayat Inayat-Khan

First of all, this practice develops the voice. It stretches the vocal cords. Most people only use a little portion of their voice, and all the rest is just slumbering. Everything that we have, though, has been given to be used, but we do not always use every function which has been granted to us by the Divine. Of course one might say, we are not all singers, so why should we develop the voice? Yet it is with the voice that we communicate with others. It is the voice that communicates the thought.

We know very well that a thought can be understood either in a right way or in a wrong way. according to the sound of the voice when the thought is communicated. One can say something with a smiling voice, and the same thing with a grumbling voice, and this will have a completely different impact on the person who hears it, although it is the same thought. The development of the voice, aside from what it means to singers, is in fact one of the techniques at our disposal with which we can convey whatever our personality has to offer. The voice is one of the many charms of the personality of the one who has made an effort to transform the rough ego into a beautiful jewel, whose radiance gladdens others.

Another important aspect of the Chromatic Zikar is that it is also a breathing exercise. When doing it, we are breathing out through the mouth, and we know that breathing out through the mouth means expelling our negative vibrations, not only of the mind, but also the physical toxins. Furthermore the Chromatic Zikar is a mind technique, because when co-ordinating the breath with the muscular action of the vocal cords to produce a given note, one is really making use of concentration. It is the mind that says to the breath and all the muscles involved, now, you go here, and you go there, and you go elsewhere.

The mind is working on the breath and is focusing it on to a given pitch when singing this or that note. It is a voluntary act, not an involuntary act. One wills the connection between the breath, the mind and the vocal cords. This is a completely co-ordinated concentration.

When we add to the Chromatic Zikar the technique of staring at a given dot, do we really realise what we are doing? It looks so simple, but in reality we are experiencing a spiritual exercise. We are discovering that between the dot and the brain there is a connection, like an invisible wire. What is that wire made of? It is made out of all those little vibrating particles of the mind, which manifest as a ray of vibration between the mind and that dot upon which we are focusing. It is a luminous ray, and if, when doing this practice, we can become consicous of that luminous ray, it becomes a very precious spiritual exercise. We are setting the chakras alight.

www.ingramcontent.com/pod-product-compliance
Lightning Source LLC
Chambersburg PA
CBHW020242090426
42735CB00010B/1801